RUBANK Treasures
for TRUMPET

ONLINE MEDIA INCLUDED
Audio Recordings
Printable Piano Accompaniments

PLAYBACK+
Speed · Pitch · Balance · Loop

T0081577

CONTENTS

To access recordings and PDF piano accompaniments, go to:
www.halleonard.com/mylibrary

Enter Code
6049-0177-8555-8168

ISBN 978-1-4803-5249-0

RUBANK®

HAL•LEONARD®
7777 W. BLUEMOUND RD. P.O. BOX 13819 MILWAUKEE, WI 53213

Visit Hal Leonard Online at
www.halleonard.com

Legend

Bb Trumpet

Vyacheslav Shchyolokov
(V. Shelukov)
Edited by William Gower

In the Hall of the Mountain King

from *Peer Gynt Suite*

Bb Trumpet

Edvard Grieg
Arranged by G.E. Holmes

00121437

American Patrol

1st B♭ Trumpet (Solo)

F.W. Meacham
Arranged by Herman A. Hummel

Tempo di Marcia
Piano

mf

(7)   (11)

(15)   1   2

(19)   (23)

f

(27)   (31)   1

mf-f   f

2   (35)   (39)

mf

(43)   (47)

(51)

f

(55)   (59)

mf

(63)

f

00121437

American Patrol

2nd B♭ Trumpet (Duet)

F.W. Meacham
Arranged by Herman A. Hummel

00121437

Allegro

B♭ Trumpet

Leroy Ostransky

00121442

Andante Cantabile

B♭ Trumpet

Guiseppe Tartini
Transcribed by H. Voxman

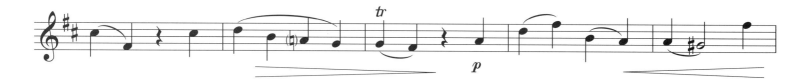

Ave Maria
(Ellens Gesang III, D. 839)

B♭ Trumpet

Franz Schubert
Arranged by Clair W. Johnson

00121437

Alleluja
from *Exsultate, Jubilate, K. 165*

Bb Trumpet

W.A. Mozart
Arranged by Clair W. Johnson

* Trills may be omitted.

Debonnaire

Bb Trumpet

Hale A. VanderCook

Allegro

f Piano

Pompously

TRIO

f

(pno.)

rit.   f   mp   a tempo

Allegro

Piano   rit.

D. S. al ⊕

CODA

Cadenza

Vivace

f

* Two clicks here signal the
piano entrance on the
following note (fermata).

Beguine and Bop

Bb Trumpet

Harold L. Walters

Achilles

B♭ Trumpet

R.M. Endresen

L'Allegro
(The Merry Man)

Bb Trumpet

Paul Koepke

* Designates a recording "click"
(accomp. recording only)

00121437

Orientale

Bb Trumpet

J.Ed. Barat
Edited by H. Voxman

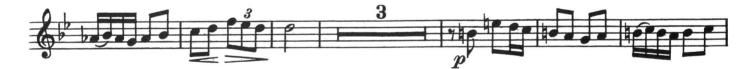

Concert Aria
"Der liebe himmlisches Gefühl," K. 382h

Bb Trumpet

W.A. Mozart
Transcribed by H. Voxman

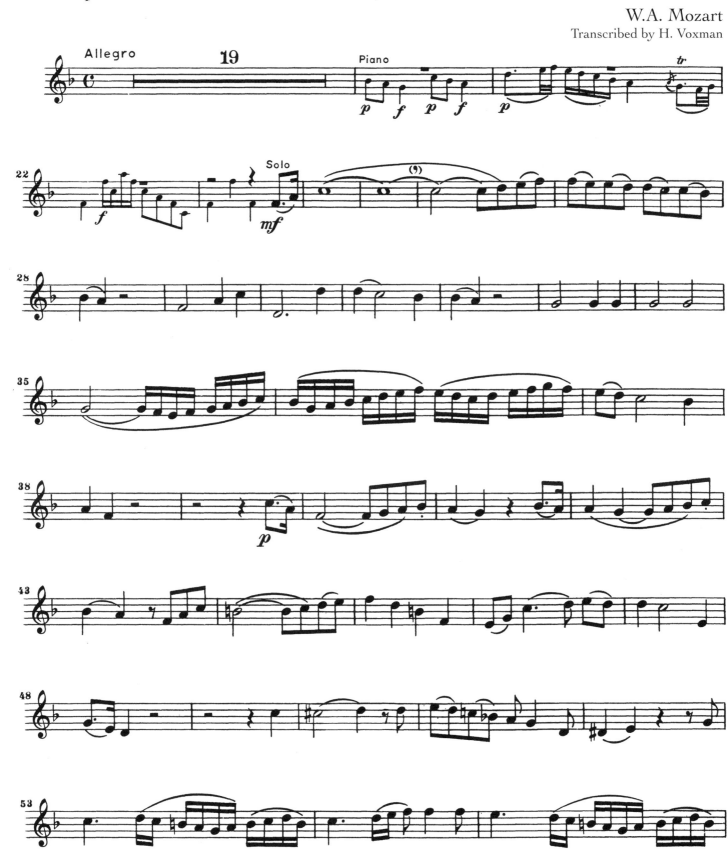

00121437

24